Dear Parent:
Your child's love of reading starts here!

Every child learns to read in a different way and at his or her own speed. Some go back and forth between reading levels and read favorite books again and again. Others read through each level in order. You can help your young reader improve and become more confident by encouraging his or her own interests and abilities. From books your child reads with you to the first books he or she reads alone, there are I Can Read Books for every stage of reading:

SHARED READING
Basic language, word repetition, and whimsical illustrations, ideal for sharing with your emergent reader

BEGINNING READING
Short sentences, familiar words, and simple concepts for children eager to read on their own

READING WITH HELP
Engaging stories, longer sentences, and language play for developing readers

READING ALONE
Complex plots, challenging vocabulary, and high-interest topics for the independent reader

ADVANCED READING
Short paragraphs, chapters, and exciting themes for the perfect bridge to chapter books

I Can Read Books have introduced children to the joy of reading since 1957. Featuring award-winning authors and illustrators and a fabulous cast of beloved characters, I Can Read Books set the standard for beginning readers.

A lifetime of discovery begins with the magical words **"I Can Read!"**

Visit www.icanread.com for information
on enriching your child's reading experience.

For Terry Stuckey and the children of Chaffee Trail
Elementary School, Jacksonville, Florida —S.M.

The author would like to thank Dr. John Durban, National Marine Fisheries
Service, NOAA, and David Mizejewski, naturalist, the National Wildlife
Federation, for sharing their enthusiasm and expertise.

The National Wildlife Federation and Ranger Rick contributors: Children's
Publication Staff and Licensing Staff.

Ranger Rick: I Wish I Was an Orca
The National Wildlife Federation.
Copyright © 2017 All rights reserved.
Manufactured in China. No part of this book may be used or reproduced in any manner whatsoever without
written permission except in the case of brief quotations embodied in critical articles and reviews. For
information address HarperCollins Children's Books, a division of HarperCollins Publishers, 195 Broadway,
New York, NY 10007.
www.icanread.com
www.RangerRick.com

Library of Congress Control Number: 2017930903
ISBN 978-0-06-243208-7 (trade bdg.) — ISBN 978-0-06-243207-0 (pbk.)

Typography by Brenda E. Angelilli

17 18 19 20 21 SCP 10 9 8 7 6 5 4 3 2 1 ❖ First Edition

Ranger Rick

I Wish I Was an Orca

by Sandra Markle

HARPER

An Imprint of HarperCollinsPublishers

What if you wished you were an orca?

Then you became an orca.

(An orca is an amazing kind of whale!)

Could you eat like an orca?

Sleep like an orca?

Live in an orca family?

And would you want to?

Find out!

Where would you live?

Orcas live in oceans

around the world,

even in the waters by Antarctica.

Would you like to live in the ocean?

Some orcas feed on only fish.

They usually find enough

to eat close to shore.

Others feed on seals and whales

that travel through the ocean.

Those orcas may feed near shore.

More often their food chase

takes them farther.

What would your family be like?

Orcas live in groups.

Each group is called a pod.

Pods are made up
of several families.

Orcas stay with their pod
their whole lives.

Would you have fun living in a pod?

An orca dives as it swims.
It often comes to the surface,
because it breathes air.
An orca breathes through a blowhole
on top of its head.
Muscles keep the blowhole closed
when the orca is underwater.

How would you learn to be an orca?

A younger calf swims

alongside its mother.

Orca calves learn

by copying what the adults do.

A calf learns to poke its head
up out of the water.
That's called spy-hopping.
Orcas spy-hop to see what's
above the water.

Young calves practice leaping
out of the water.

Leaping helps orcas swim fast.

Older calves play together.

They leap over one another.

They also play

by pushing their tails up

and slapping them down hard.

SPLASH! SPLASH! SPLASH!

How would you talk?

Orcas talk with clicks.

They also whistle and squeak.

Each pod has its own way

of using sounds to talk.

Calves copy their mothers

to learn to talk to their pod.

What if your family had its own special way of talking?

Pods use teamwork to hunt.

Calves join in to learn what to do.

Sometimes orcas use

their clicking sounds to hunt.

Sound waves hit schools of fish

and bounce back as echoes.

That's how orcas hunt in dark waters.

Would it be handy to use echoes to find objects you couldn't see?

What would you eat?

A calf drinks its mother's milk
for the first two years of its life.
The rich milk helps the calf
grow a layer of fat called blubber.
The blubber keeps an orca warm
in cold ocean waters.

Orca calves have a full set of teeth
when they are born.
Each tooth is long and sharp.
Calves will use these teeth
to catch food when they are older.
Orcas share meals.
Food sharing is a big part
of being a family.

Where would you sleep?

Orcas sleep in the ocean.

While resting, orcas swim slowly

and stay close to each other.

When an orca rests,

only half of its brain goes to sleep.

The other half stays alert

so the whale can swim to the surface

to breathe while it is sleeping.

Would you like to swim while you sleep?

How would growing up change you?

As the calves get older,

they grow bigger.

Males grow to around

22 feet (6.7 meters) long.

Females are usually a little smaller.

Would you like to grow up that fast?

Males also grow a bigger dorsal

fin than the females.

The dorsal fin is the tall fin on their backs.

By age five, the calves help

the other orcas in the pod hunt.

Being an orca could be cool for a while.

But would you want to live in the ocean?

Swim while you sleep?

Or eat only meat when you grow up?

Luckily, you don't have to.

You're not an orca.

You're YOU!

Did You Know?

🐾 A newborn orca weighs over 300 pounds (136 kilograms) and can be 8 feet (2.4 meters) long.

🐾 Scientists believe some orcas may be nearly 100 years old.

🐾 Orcas can swim as fast as 28 miles per hour (45 kilometers per hour). But they can only do that for short bursts. Orcas usually swim about 8 miles per hour (12.8 kilometers per hour). That's about twice as fast as people can swim.

🐾 Orcas sometimes work together to make waves that can knock seals off chunks of floating ice.

🐾 Most people call orcas killer whales. But orcas hunt only for food.

When an orca wants to find things in the ocean it can't see, it makes some clicking sounds.
If the sounds hit something in front of the orca, they bounce back as echoes. By listening to the echoes, an orca can tell how far away something is.

You may not have a way to hear echoes, but you can still get a feel for how sounds help an orca find something in the dark.

Can you zero in on sounds? Get a friend to work with you and follow these steps to find out.

Stand in the middle of an open area and close your eyes. Have your friend stay an arm's length away and circle around you.

Get ready!

Start making clicking noises. Your friend should softly echo those clicks while circling around you. Can you zero in on those echoes to reach out and grab your friend?

Was it easy or hard to do?

Repeat two more times. With practice, did you do better using echoes to find your friend?

Orca calves practice making clicks and listening before they join in pod hunts.

Wild Words

Blowhole: the opening on top of an orca's head through which it breathes

Blubber: the layer of fat under an orca's skin that helps it stay warm in cold water

Calf: a baby orca

Dorsal fin: the fin on top of an orca's back

Spy-hopping: when an orca pokes its head out of the water to look around

Dig Deeper
WANT TO FIND OUT EVEN MORE ABOUT ORCAS?
Check out the Ranger Rick website: www.RangerRick.com
SEARCH: orcas

Photo Credits: Hysazu Photography, Alaska Fisheries Science Center, NOAA Fisheries Service: Thomas Jefferson, Janice Waite, Kim Parsons, Holly Fearnbach and David Ellifrit, Getty Images: Sethakan, Vladsilver, Troutnut, Rasmus-Raahauge, Jeff Foott, Rebecca-Belleni-Photography.